STANDARD DEDUCTION

Filing Status	1994 Amount
Married individuals filing joint returns and surviving spouses	$6,350
Heads of households	5,600
Unmarried individuals (other than surviving spouses and heads of households)	3,800
Married individuals filing separate return	3,175
Additional standard deductions for the aged and the blind	
Individual who is married and surviving spouses	750*
Individual who is unmarried and not a surviving spouse	950*
Taxpayer claimed as dependent on another taxpayer's return	600

These amounts are $1,500 and $1,900, respectively, for a taxpayer who is both aged and blind.

Personal Exemption   1994: $2,450**

****Reduction in personal and dependency exemptions*

The personal and dependency exemption deductions are reduced or eliminated for certain high-income taxpayers. When a taxpayer's AGI exceeds the "phaseout begins after" amount described below, the deduction is reduced by 2% for each $2,500 (or fraction thereof) by which AGI exceeds such amount. For married persons filing separately, the exemption deduction is reduced by 2% for each $1,250 (or fraction thereof) by which AGI exceeds the "phaseout begins after" amount. The personal exemption deduction amount cannot be reduced below zero.

The phaseout ranges are:

Filing Status	Phaseout Begins After	Phaseout Completed After
Married individuals filing joint return and surviving spouses	$167,700	$290,200
Heads of households	139,750	262,250
Unmarried taxpayers (other than surviving spouses and heads of households)	111,800	234,300
Married individuals filing separate returns	83,850	145,100

Itemized Deductions

The itemized deductions that are otherwise deductible for the tax year are reduced by the lesser of (1) 3% of the excess of AGI over a threshold amount, or (2) 80% of the amount of itemized deductions otherwise deductible for the tax year excluding medical expenses, investment interest expense, casualty losses, and wagering losses to the extent of wagering gains. The threshold amount for the 1994 tax year is $111,800 (except for married individuals filing separate returns for which it is $55,900).

PRENTICE HALL'S FEDERAL TAXATION, 1995

Individuals

Editors

LAWRENCE C. PHILLIPS
University of Miami

JOHN L. KRAMER
University of Florida

Co-authors

D. DALE BANDY
University of Central Florida

N. ALLEN FORD
University of Kansas

ROBERT L. GARDNER
Brigham Young University

Annotations by

W. PETER SALZARULO
Miami University of Ohio

PRENTICE HALL, Englewood Cliffs, New Jersey 07632

Editorial/production supervision: Kristin E. Dackow
Managing editor: Robert Dewey
Editorial Assistant: Amy Hinton
Interior design: Levavi & Levavi, Inc.
Cover design: Richard Stalzer/Bruce Kenselaar
Manufacturing buyer: Herb Klein

ISSN 0898-2627

Printed in the United States of America
10 9 8 7 6 5 4 3 2 1

ISBN 0-13-098930-4
ISBN 0-13-098948-7 (IE)

Prentice-Hall International (UK) Limited, *London*
Prentice-Hall of Australia Pty. Limited, *Sydney*
Prentice-Hall Canada Inc., *Toronto*
Prentice-Hall Hispanoamericana, S.A., *Mexico*
Prentice-Hall of India Private Limited, *New Delhi*
Prentice-Hall of Japan, Inc., *Tokyo*
Prentice-Hall of Southeast Asia Pte. Ltd., *Singapore*
Editora Prentice-Hall do Brasil, Ltda., *Rio de Janeiro*